THE
KWAKIUTL
INDIANS

THE JUNIOR LIBRARY OF
AMERICAN INDIANS

THE
KWAKIUTL
INDIANS

G. S. Prentzas

CHELSEA HOUSE PUBLISHERS
New York   Philadelphia

FRONTISPIECE: A Kwakiutl chief speaking at a potlatch hosted by anthropologist Franz Boas in 1894

CHAPTER TITLE ORNAMENT: A Raven crest symbol from a Kwakiutl graveyard in Alert Bay, British Columbia

Chelsea House Publishers
EDITOR-IN-CHIEF Richard S. Papale
MANAGING EDITOR Karyn Gullen Browne
COPY CHIEF Philip Koslow
PICTURE EDITOR Adrian G. Allen
ART DIRECTOR Nora Wertz
MANUFACTURING DIRECTOR Gerald Levine
SYSTEMS MANAGER Lindsey Ottman
PRODUCTION COORDINATOR Marie Claire Cebrián-Ume

The Junior Library of American Indians
SENIOR EDITOR Liz Sonneborn

Staff for THE KWAKIUTL INDIANS
ASSOCIATE EDITOR Martin Schwabacher
COPY EDITOR David Carter
EDITORIAL ASSISTANT Nicole Greenblatt
DESIGNER Debora Smith
PICTURE RESEARCHER Pat Burns
COVER ILLUSTRATOR Vilma Ortiz

Library of Congress Cataloging-in-Publication Data

Prentzas, G. S.
  The Kwakiutl Indians/by G. S. Prentzas
  p. cm.—(The Junior Library of American Indians)
  Includes index.
Summary: Examines the life and culture of the Kwakiutl Indians.
  ISBN 0-7910-1664-1
  ISBN 0-7910-1959-4 (pbk.)
1. Kwakiutl Indians—Juvenile literature. [1. Kwakiutl Indians.
2. Indians of North America—British Columbia.] I. Title. II. Series.
E99.K9P74 1993   92-18431
971.1'004979—dc20   CIP
                                                          AC

CONTENTS

A chief wearing the crest image of an animal spirit.

CHAPTER **1**

The First People

Long ago, Raven flew down to earth from the upper world, the home of sun, moon, and stars. After he landed on the ground, he began to explore. He walked up and down the beach. But soon Raven became bored and cried out to the upper world.

The heavens answered with a soft, low groan. Raven looked all around. At his feet, he found a huge shell. It cracked open a little, and Raven saw that the shell was full of tiny creatures, who were peeking out at him.

Raven tried to convince the terrified beings to come out of their shell and play with him. One of the strange creatures bravely left the safety of the shell. Another followed. Soon Raven was surrounded by a group of feather-less, two-legged beings. They had pale skin and were naked except for the long, black hair on their heads. Instead of wings, they had long, sticklike arms. Raven was glad to have these new playmates—the first people.

At first the people were cold and hungry, but Raven gave them everything they needed to live comfortably. From the upper world, he stole daylight, fire, and fresh water. He made rivers and filled them with salmon.

After giving his people many other gifts, Raven shouted loudly. He wanted to find out if anyone else lived on the earth. He was answered by the calls of Wolf, Grizzly Bear, Mink, and others. They, too, had found people.

The story of Raven and the origin of humans is one of many told by the Kwakiutls. The name Kwakiutl (pronounced approxi-mately KWA-gee-oolth) refers to the Indians who lived along the northern and eastern shores of Vancouver Island and the nearby mainland of British Columbia, Canada. Like other coastal Indians of the Pacific Northwest, the Kwakiutls made their living by fishing in the ocean and rivers.

Studying the Kwakiutls' traditional stories is one way to learn about how they viewed the world. These tales often show the links between the Kwakiutls, their ancestors, and animals. Most Kwakiutl families trace their origin to a spirit. Many of these spirits took on the form of animals such as Raven. They could grant a family the right to fish or pick berries in a special place, or even give them magic powers. Each family had its own dances and songs that told the story of how the spirit helped them.

Another way to learn about the Kwakiutls is to study the work of *anthropologists*. Anthropologists are scientists who try to understand how different people live. Sometimes anthropologists examine tools and other objects that a group of people made long ago. At other times, they actually visit a people and watch them carefully, observing what they do and listening to what they say.

Many of the first white people to come to the Kwakiutls' land were cruel to the Indians. One man called them "the most hideous . . . beings imaginable." Another described them as "dirty greasy nasty-smelling savages." But one early visitor—an anthropologist named Franz Boas—treated them with respect.

Boas was greatly impressed by the Kwakiutls, especially with their art and religious rituals. He found them to be a proud people with an extremely complex society.

LOCATIONS OF MAJOR KWAKIUTL VILLAGES

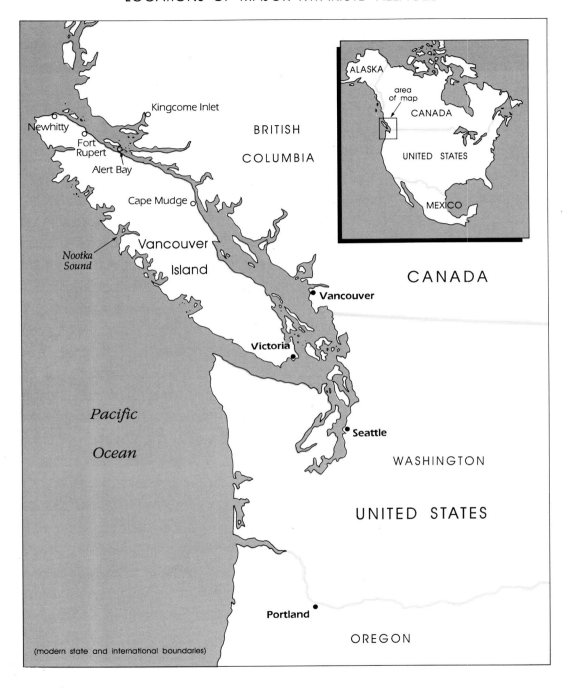

Kingcome Inlet

Newhitty

Fort Rupert

Alert Bay

BRITISH COLUMBIA

Cape Mudge

Vancouver Island

Nootka Sound

CANADA

● Vancouver

Victoria ●

Pacific

Ocean

● Seattle

WASHINGTON

UNITED STATES

Portland ●

OREGON

(modern state and international boundaries)

ALASKA

area of map

CANADA

UNITED STATES

MEXICO

Every family had a specific rank and worked hard to increase its status and honor.

To keep their high rank, wealthier families had to invite their neighbors to special feasts called *potlatches*. The hosts made speeches, performed songs and dances about their ancestors, and gave away gifts. A large potlatch, where many gifts were given away, would be sung about at future potlatches for generations.

Franz Boas visited the Kwakiutls for the first time in 1886 at the village of Newhitty. By that time, the Canadian government had passed a law prohibiting all Northwest Coast Indians from holding potlatches. The Newhitty Kwakiutls refused to obey the law, so the government threatened to send a gunboat to destroy their village. Boas gave a speech at a potlatch explaining that he was on the Indians' side:

> I do not wish to interfere with your celebration. My people live far away and would like to know what people in distant lands do. . . . I shall go back and say: "See, that is how the people there live. They were good to me and asked me to live with them."

Boas invited the Indians to his own potlatch before he left. Near the end of the ceremony, a great chief made a speech. Pointing to Boas, he said: "This chief has come to us from a distant land, and all our hearts are glad. He is not like the other whites who have come to us. . . . We are glad he came and hope he will return."

Boas did return, many times. The Indians rewarded him by giving him a Kwakiutl name and showing him their secrets. In 1894, he was invited to attend the mysterious *Winter Ceremonial*. Boas was amazed by what he saw.

The Kwakiutls believed that during their winter ceremonies, powerful spirits came to visit them. The spirits captured young people and gave them magic powers. While under the spirits' power, the young people acted wild. The purpose of the ceremony was to tame the possessed youths.

Boas watched in wonder as an untamed boy danced wildly before him, lunging at the audience. He was being initiated into the secret society of the Cannibal-at-the-North-End-of-the-World. This spirit had mouths all over his body and ate human flesh. While possessed by a cannibal spirit, the dancer had to be guarded or he too would try to bite people. Sometimes he even drew blood.

It took four days to tame the dancer. Afterward the people who had been bitten were paid. Boas later learned that they had agreed to pretend to be bitten beforehand. The entire

Anthropologist Franz Boas, wearing a bark blanket, poses as a Kwakiutl Indian for artists at the Smithsonian Institution. A life-size diorama of the Kwakiutls' hamatsa ceremony was made from these poses.

performance had been carefully planned. These shows were so convincing, however, that some early European visitors thought the Kwakiutls were really cannibals.

Boas discovered that the Kwakiutls loved magic tricks, which were used to show the magic powers of the spirits. In one trick, a dancer representing Tooquid, a female warrior spirit, told the audience to kill her. On-lookers appeared to pound a stake into her head, and blood seemed to pour from the wound. This trick was done by secretly breaking bags of seal blood on her head.

Another magic trick was performed by the Thrower of Sickness. He had a magic stick that could change lengths. At one point in the ceremony, he threw it over the audience's

These Kwakiutls fish in the same waters their ancestors did thousands of years ago.

heads. When they looked back, the stick was floating in the air, vibrating. Actually, what they saw was a different stick, hung from strings and shaken by the dancer's assistants.

Boas and other anthropologists who followed him wrote about these fantastic rituals. If they had not, many old Kwakiutl ways would be lost forever. As the years passed, more and more whites moved to the Pacific Northwest. They took most of the Kwakiutls' land and forced them to live like white people.

But the Kwakiutls continued some of their rituals in secret. Today, their ceremonies are legal again, and Kwakiutl culture is being revived. Elders give lessons in Kwakiutl language, dancing, and woodcarving to the young people. Many still live and fish in the same places their ancestors have for thousands of years. ▲

The Kwakiutl village of Alert Bay in the late 1800s.

CHAPTER 2

The Land of Salmon and Cedar

Twenty thousand years ago, no people lived in North America. Large masses of ice known as glaciers descended from the north and covered much of the continent. During this ice age, a land bridge between North America and Asia appeared where the water had been. People from Asia walked over the bridge. These were the first human beings in America.

The ancestors of the Kwakiutl Indians settled on the Northwest Coast, just north of the present-day state of Washington. At first they hunted in the forest and ate whatever vegetables and berries they could find. But when the ice finished melting, fish and shellfish became plentiful. The Indians could catch all the fish they needed and still devote a great deal of time to religion, magic, art, and ceremonies.

The Kwakiutls lived in a special environment. The mild temperatures and heavy rainfall of the Pacific Northwest created a thick forest of towering trees. A heavy tangle of shrubs and bushes made walking through the forest almost impossible. Although the Kwakiutls sometimes went into the forest to collect wood or hunt, their lives centered on the sea.

The cold, deep, murky waters of the northern Pacific Coast are one of the world's greatest fishing grounds. The most important fish to the Kwakiutls were salmon, which live in the ocean but swim up rivers each year to lay their eggs. The Kwakiutls caught and ate fresh salmon during the summer. The fish that was not eaten was preserved and saved for winter meals.

Other fish the Kwakiutls caught were herring, smelt, cod, and eulachon (OO-la-ken). Of these, the eulachon—also known as the candlefish—was the one most prized by the Kwakiutls. The bodies of the eulachon contained so much fat that if a wick were placed in one's mouth and lit, the fish would burn like a candle. The Kwakiutls often dipped their food in a small bowl of eulachon oil.

Besides fish, the Kwakiutls hunted many other kinds of sea animals, including seals, porpoises, sea otters, and seabirds. They also ate crabs, octopuses, squid, sea urchins, and other seafood.

Many animals lived in the woods, but the thick brush made it hard to hunt on land. The Kwakiutls did hunt deer and elk with bows

This cedar-bark basket was used to carry fish.

and arrows. They also baited traps to catch grizzly bears, black bears, and wolves. Small animals such as beavers and minks were caught for their fur.

The Kwakiutls collected bulbs, roots, and the leaves of ferns, skunk cabbage, and other plants to add to their meals. They picked blackberries, huckleberries, crabapples, and other fruits that they found in the forest. But their most important food was fish.

Because they relied so much on salmon and other fish, the Kwakiutls invented many ways to catch them. Men used nets to catch fish in slow, deep waters. Larger fish were caught with hooks and lines. But the best tools for salmon fishing were wooden fences known as weirs and stone traps. Both were built across streams to trap the fish. Some weirs channeled the fish through smaller and smaller boxes and tubes until they could no longer turn around.

In spring, eulachon and herring swam near the shore in large schools. The Kwakiutls caught them with big dip nets or with special rakes. Fishermen combed the rakes through the water to spear the fish.

The Kwakiutls gathered enough food in the summer months to last the whole year. But they could not have survived if they had not learned how to dry and preserve food for the

A door painted to repre-sent the mouth of an animal spirit. The Kwa-kiutls believed they could be spiritually transformed by entering a house through such a door.

winter, when storms made fishing difficult. During the fishing season, boneless strips of fish were hung on slats of wood to dry in the sun. Smokehouses, special huts for preserving meat, were filled with fish to dry above the heat of a fire. Some kinds of fish and other foods were mixed with eulachon oil or seal oil to keep them from spoiling.

In summer, the Kwakiutls grilled and baked fresh fish. In winter, strips of dried fish were boiled in water, which helped restore moisture to the fish. To boil food, the Indians placed it in a box or basket filled with water and then dropped in red-hot stones.

Fishing was possible only at a few spots along the steep and rocky coast. Because these areas were usually not good places to live year-round, the Kwakiutls stayed only for the summer fishing season. They built temporary villages from cedar planks that they took off their larger winter houses. When the fishing season was over, they carried these planks back to rebuild their winter homes.

In winter, the Kwakiutls lived in villages sheltered from the high winter tides and fierce storms. Their villages consisted of rows of wooden houses that were sometimes built on stilts. A boardwalk ran in front of the houses for the entire length of the village.

The Kwakiutls liked big houses. A large winter house might be 100 feet long, 40 feet wide, and 20 feet high. Several related families lived in each house. Plank or mat walls separated each family's living area. The head of the household and his immediate family always lived along the house's rear wall. The other families lived along the side and front walls, depending on their rank. The center of the house was open and contained a cooking fire that everyone used.

A cedar pole erected outside the house, known as a *totem pole*, showed the status of the family who lived inside. Totem poles

A totem pole outside a house in Alert Bay, photographed in 1895.

were carved and sometimes painted with *crest symbols*, images of humans, animals, and supernatural beings or spirits to whom the family was spiritually connected. The poles told the story of important events in the mythic history of the family.

Totem poles were thought to link humans to the spirit world. Prayers to the spirits could be addressed to totem poles. The Kwakiutls often placed small offerings of food and tobacco in front of them. They sometimes recarved or repainted the poles to renew the relationships between humans and spirits.

There were several types of totem poles. The largest were 30 to 50 feet high and stood in front of a house. Sometimes they were attached to the house, and the mouth of an animal carved on the pole was used as a door during ceremonies.

Another type was the memorial pole, a 20-to-30-foot pole built in honor of a chief who had died. These poles had only a few carved or painted figures, which showed the chief and symbols of his life. The raising of the memorial pole was accompanied by a potlatch. During this special ceremony, the new chief would take over the dead chief's titles.

Interior house posts were the most common type of totem pole. They were carved from the large timbers that supported the roof. These poles were also decorated with crest symbols. Often the figures carved on totem poles were shown holding a *copper*, the Kwakiutls' most important ceremonial object.

The Kwakiutls made a wide variety of things from trees. The forest contained many types of trees, but the red cedar was the most important to the Kwakiutls. In addition to houses and totem poles, red cedar wood was used to make storage containers, canoes, cradles, weapons, and ceremonial items. From the tree's soft inner bark, the Indians made clothing, baskets, ropes, and mats.

The Kwakiutls were well known for their wooden containers. Using steam and carefully cut grooves, they could fold a single piece of wood to form all four sides of a box. They then sewed on a bottom that fit so tightly that the box could hold water.

Wooden boxes and bowls were used to store food and family valuables. They also served as furniture, as platters, and even as coffins. Boxes and bowls used during ceremonies were often carved in the shape of animals.

Perhaps the most important wooden object made by the Kwakiutls was the canoe. They would not have been able to live on the

This canoe was made from the trunk of a single cedar tree. Canoes used for trade or war expeditions could carry up to 50 people.

coast without a way to travel on water. The Kwakiutls made canoes of many different sizes and shapes. Their smallest canoes were one- or two-person boats used for river voyages. Their largest canoes could carry as many as 50 people.

A canoe maker created a canoe from a single cedar log—a long and difficult job. First, he chopped down a very tall cedar. He then split the log in half lengthwise. Using one of the halves, the maker shaped the outside of the canoe. After charring the wood with hot rocks, he hollowed out the inside with chisels and an adz, a cutting tool similar to an ax. The canoe was then filled with hot water and carefully bent into shape. It was sanded smooth, then covered with dogfish oil to make it waterproof. Finally, the vessel was painted and decorated.

Like all Kwakiutl activities, canoe making

involved religious rituals. A carver spent a great deal of time praying and singing sacred songs. A canoe and the tree from which it was made were thought to be alive and to have a soul.

Kwakiutl women made many types of baskets. Most were used to carry or store food and other objects. A skilled basket maker could weave one so tightly that it was waterproof. These baskets made good rain hats. Baskets for everyday use were not decorated. Those made to hold special things were adorned with patterns or animal designs.

Mats woven from cedar bark and other fibers were used as rugs, cushions, and even clothing. During cold and wet weather, the Kwakiutls needed warm, water-repellent clothes. The most common garment was a woven cedar-bark blanket. They wrapped the blankets around their bodies and tied or pinned them shut.

During the summer, the Kwakiutls wore few clothes. Men often wore just a *breech-cloth* or nothing at all. Women usually wore only a small skirt. Most of the time, people went barefoot.

Living in an area with so many natural resources, the Kwakiutls were able to feed, shelter, and clothe themselves easily. Their lives were relatively comfortable, and they were able to devote most of their time to art, religion, and rituals. However, when the Kwakiutls first encountered European traders in 1792, their society changed forever. ▲

A woman softens strips of cedar bark, which she will weave into a blanket like the one she is wearing.

A man wearing rope armor and clothing made of cedar bark.

CHAPTER 3

Strangers Arrive

The first non-Indians to come to the Kwakiutls' land were fur traders. Beaver fur was in great demand in Europe. The soft fur was made into warm, waterproof clothing and hats. These items were so popular that hunters eventually killed most of the beavers and other furry animals living in Europe and Asia.

When European explorers sent home reports that fur-bearing animals were plentiful in North America, the news was greeted with excitement. In the early 1600s, English and French fur traders sailed across the Atlantic Ocean to the eastern coast of North America. There they found all the beaver furs that

29

they wanted. At the same time, Russian fur traders sailed across the Pacific Ocean to Alaska.

From Alaska, the Russian traders traveled south down the Pacific coast. Many fur-bearing animals lived on the Northwest Coast, including sea otters, whose pelts were treasured in Asia. But the Tlingits (TLING-kits), a native group that lived north of the Kwa-kiutls, fought to keep the traders out of their territory. After several bloody battles, the Russians left.

The arrival of Captain James Cook and his crew in Nootka Sound in 1778, as drawn by John Webber, the ship's official artist.

European traders tried to reach the Northwest Coast from California, to the south of the Kwakiutls' land. But rough waters, fog, and strong winds made it difficult to sail along the coast north of San Francisco. In the late 1700s, an easy-to-sail route to the region was found via Hawaii. With this discovery, the fur trade in the Pacific Northwest began in earnest.

In the summer of 1778, the English explorer James Cook visited the Nootkas, who lived near the Kwakiutls. Captain Cook and his crew sailed into Nootka Sound and stayed for a month. Many hundreds of Indians came to see Cook's ship. Because the Kwakiutls and the Nootkas were trading partners, some Kwakiutls were probably present. If so, this was the Kwakiutls' first contact with the Europeans.

Cook and his crew traded glass beads, clothing, knives, and pieces of iron to the Indians for about 1,500 sea otter pelts. The Englishmen later sold the furs in China for an immense profit. Each pelt had cost them about 10 cents, but in China they sold for about $100. At that time, $100 was nearly 10 times what a sailor earned in an entire year.

When they heard of the money to be made in sea otter furs, hundreds of traders set sail from England and Boston. Within a few years of Cook's return to England, there were ships trading all along the Northwest coast. Furs bought from the Indians for a few chisel blades or other European goods could be traded in China for a fortune in silk, furniture, porcelain, spices, and tea. One successful voyage might mean a lifetime of wealth and luxury for a crafty trader.

The first Europeans known to visit a Kwakiutl village were the crew of an English ship, the *Chatham*. This vessel, commanded by George Vancouver, visited the Kwakiutls at Cape Mudge in 1792. The journals of the ship's officers provide the first written description of the Kwakiutl people.

In the journal of the ship's doctor, the Kwakiutls are described as slender, short-limbed, and of medium height. The doctor wrote that they had flat faces, small eyes, and small, poorly maintained teeth. Their faces were painted with red-and-black designs. They wore copper and shell ornaments in holes pierced in their earlobes and noses, and their hair was decorated with red ocher (a clay high in iron ore), soot, and birds' down.

Vancouver and his crew soon departed from Cape Mudge and sailed north. On July 19, 1792, they sighted a large Kwakiutl village near Alert Bay. The village had 34 houses, some of which were decorated with painted figures. Between 350 and 500 people lived there.

The next morning, a group of Kwakiutl Indians paddled their canoes out to the ship and invited the English ashore. When the visitors arrived on the beach, they were welcomed with a large, formal greeting ceremony. The Indians then began to trade with their guests. The chief took charge of the exchange of sea otter pelts. He allowed villagers to swap pelts for beads, buttons, and other trinkets for themselves. Vancouver wrote in his journal that the Kwakiutls were smart traders.

The Kwakiutls obtained many different types of European goods from the fur traders. At first, they mostly traded for metal, especially iron and copper. They used iron to make tools and weapons. They made jewelry and ceremonial items from copper. Later, the Indians bargained for cloth, tools, mirrors, cooking pots, and such foodstuffs as flour, rice, tea, and sugar.

Whenever a trading ship dropped anchor near a native village, it was greeted by a fleet of canoes. A leader performed a dance on a platform in the largest canoe and sprinkled red ocher or eagles' down on the water. These actions showed he came in peace. The Kwakiutls then performed many long

rituals, which included speeches, dancing, singing, and the presentation of gifts.

These ceremonies were sometimes performed for days before trading began. To the Kwakiutls, such rituals were as important as the actual exchange of goods. The long ceremonies, however, annoyed the white traders. They were eager to finish trading with one village and quickly move on to the next.

Although Indian and white traders sometimes cheated or robbed each other, their relations were usually peaceful. The nature

Painting of a Canadian sea otter by American artist John James Audubon. In the 1700s, non-Indian traders flocked to the Northwest Coast in search of sea otter furs.

of fur trading changed, however, when several companies set up permanent trading posts in the region. They began competing with the trading ships for furs.

At first, the competition helped the Kwakiutls. With more white traders wanting their furs, they could ask for higher prices. But the good times for the Indians did not last long. The land-based trading companies soon ran the trading ships out of business. By 1821, the British-owned Hudson's Bay Company had bought out the other trading companies. Indians who wanted European goods now had to accept its prices.

The first trading post in Kwakiutl territory was Fort Rupert. Soon after it was built in 1849, Fort Rupert became the major hub of Kwakiutl trade. Entire villages moved to be near the fort. During the 1850s and 1860s, about 3,000 Indians lived at Fort Rupert. This was about 10 times the size of a traditional village. At the same time, Kwakiutl villages that had been centers for trading with ships lost their power and population.

Gradually, the fur trade began to change the Kwakiutl way of life. At first, Indian hunters did exactly what they had done for years. They hunted animals and traded the pelts to their friends for other goods. Within a few decades, however, the population of sea otters dropped so low that the Indians had to find new ways of getting furs.

Throughout the Pacific Northwest, Indians became more willing to trade, steal, or kill to get pelts. Before the arrival of white traders, the tribes of the Northwest Coast had sometimes fought with each other. But after fur trading became so important, warfare was constant. Armed with European and American guns, Indians sometimes wiped out entire rival villages.

Warfare also affected where Northwest Coast Indians chose to live. The Kwakiutls had always settled in small villages close to their sources of food. After the fur trade began, however, many small communities joined to form new, larger villages that were easier to defend.

Contact with the traders affected the Kwakiutls' lives in many other ways. The unfamiliar behavior of the foreign traders fascinated the Indians. Often, curious Indians sat on the ships' decks for hours at a time just to watch the strangers. Sailors taught the Indians about Christianity and urged them to adopt Christian values and beliefs. They also introduced the Kwakiutls to liquor and gambling.

Each time the Indians were introduced to a new white custom or belief, they had to decide whether to adopt it themselves. This caused conflict among the Indians. Some wanted to protect their society by resisting change. Others believed they must adapt to get along with their new neighbors.

The worst new problem the Indians faced was the deadly new diseases the sailors brought with them. Smallpox, measles, mumps, scarlet fever, and influenza soon swept through the Pacific Northwest. Many Indians died because they had never been exposed to these diseases before and so had no resistance to them.

Smallpox *epidemics* were probably the most deadly. During the 1780s and 1790s, smallpox struck several Indian groups, including the Kwakiutls. A major epidemic that lasted from 1862 to 1864 hit almost every tribe, killing one-third of the Indian population in the Pacific Northwest.

Although many of the old ways survived, the fur trade had changed the Kwakiutls' lives. They were suddenly exposed to new customs and beliefs. Many moved away from the fishing villages where their ancestors had lived for generations. And much of their population died during the epidemics.

The Kwakiutls responded to these rapid changes with intelligence and creativity. For some time, they remained firmly in control of

A Kwakiutl man on an English ship, photographed in 1873.

their own lives. As long as the newcomers wanted only furs, the Indians were left alone to hunt on their land as they wished. But the future would present them with new and even more difficult challenges. The Kwakiutls would encounter a new breed of whites—settlers hungry for control of the Kwakiutls' ancestral lands. ▲

A chief's house with
two totem poles, pho-
tographed in 1909.

CHAPTER **4**

Hard Times

In the mid-1850s, the Kwakiutls' world was rocked by an event that would change their way of life forever. Gold was discovered on their land. Thousands of miners poured into the region. In 1856 the population of Victoria, a coastal town on Vancouver Island, included about 500 whites. By the end of 1858, the number of whites had soared to 25,000.

Miners set up camps along river valleys throughout the Pacific Northwest. Many took over sites that had been Indian fishing spots for hundreds of years. Conflicts often arose. Some miners murdered Indians. Others poisoned salmon streams with mercury, a toxic metal that they used to process gold

41

ore. To the settlers, the Indians were simply in the way.

The colonial government signed treaties with some Indian groups near the Kwakiutls. It promised to give the Indians small amounts of cash and plots of land called *reserves*. The Indians would be allowed to occupy these reserves forever. In return, the Indians would give up their rights to the rest of their lands.

The English never honored these treaties. They paid the Indians only a small amount of what they had promised, and the government did not stop settlers from seizing lands that were part of the reserves. So many whites had moved to the region that the Indians no longer posed a threat to their settlements. The English soon stopped bothering to make treaties with the Indians at all.

By the early 1860s, the English government began using any means to take away land from the Indians. It sold to whites tens of thousands of acres that had been set aside as Indian reserves. In 1865, a law was passed that made it illegal for an Indian family in British Columbia to have more than 10 acres. At the same time, a white settler could own 640 acres.

More and more, the colonial government began to interfere with the daily life of the Indians. It set up a police force that was

Thousands of gold miners came to the Pacific Northwest in the 1850s.

supposed to protect Indians, but the police did not treat the Indians fairly. When Indians were robbed or murdered by whites, the police rarely tried to catch the lawbreakers. But when Indian leaders refused to hand over tribe members accused of crimes, their villages were attacked by English gunships.

The English bombarded several Kwakiutl villages. In the worst attack, naval artillery completely destroyed the village at Fort Rupert in 1865. Although the Kwakiutls built a new village a short distance away, the raid shattered the villagers' morale.

When the gold deposits in the region ran out, most of the prospectors left. But many thousands of non-Indian settlers stayed in British Columbia, which in 1871 had become a province in the new nation of Canada. Victoria, the capital of British Columbia, was by then a large city populated by Europeans, Asians, and Indians. Large numbers of Indians, including hundreds of Kwakiutls, traveled to Victoria each summer to trade their goods.

A group of Kwakiutls soon formed a permanent settlement in Victoria. They made their living by working for wages. Some became fishermen, hunters, or loggers. Others joined the crews of whaling ships. As more non-Indians settled in Victoria, Indians had a harder time finding work. They could get only the lowest-paying jobs. Most of the Kwakiutls in Victoria ended up living in an overcrowded Indian ghetto.

The Kwakiutls that remained on their lands continued many of their traditional ways. Because fewer non-Indians moved into their territory, the Kwakiutls held on to their ancestral lands longer than other neighboring groups. The Kwakiutls were proud that they still observed many of their traditions while many of their Salish, Nootka, and Haida (HI-duh) neighbors adopted white ways. The isolation of the Kwakiutls, however, did not last long.

In the 1880s, the Canadian government began breaking up Indian reserves into small plots called *allotments*. Allotments were to be owned as private property by individual families. Any part of the reserve not allotted to a family was taken by whites. For example, an Indian family might now own the land where their house stood, the place where they fished, and one berry patch, while whites owned all the land between these spots. Tens of thousands of acres were taken away and sold to non-Indian settlers.

The Kwakiutls continued to hunt and fish, but they no longer had enough land to feed themselves by gathering food in the traditional way. Most had to earn wages, usually by working as fishermen or as laborers in canneries. Jobs were hard to come by because non-Indian employers preferred hiring whites and Japanese immigrants.

To make matters worse, the government passed a series of anti-Indian laws that made the lives of all Indians in Canada much more difficult. One law denied Indians the right to vote. Another prohibited the Indians from drinking liquor. The Indian Act of 1876 made it a crime to take part in most Indian social and religious practices, including the potlatch.

Government officials known as agents were responsible for enforcing anti-Indian laws. Agents were supposed to represent the interests of Indians to government officials. Their main duty, however, was to watch for Indian uprisings and to encourage Indians to abandon their traditions.

During this period, *missionaries* arrived in British Columbia to teach the beliefs of white Canadians to Indians. The missionaries hoped that the Indians would accept Christianity. Many also wanted the Indians to adopt white ways.

The missionaries tried to stop the Indians from practicing their traditional religions. Some missionaries burned masks and other

These children, photographed in 1918, were taught to reject their native culture by Christian missionaries at a school in Nootka territory.

ritual items or talked Indian converts into destroying them. They also chopped down totem poles and painted over crest designs.

Many missionaries preached that native customs—from baby-naming ceremonies to burial rites—were sinful and evil. The missionaries made converts live in single-family dwellings instead of their large communal houses, disrupting the complex ties between families. Indian children attending mission schools were not allowed to speak their native language.

Although missionaries were less active among the Kwakiutls than other tribes, many Kwakiutls converted to Christianity during the late 1800s. For some, it was merely a way of getting into mission schools, obtaining medical care, or receiving some other form of aid. Others discovered a new, meaningful set of social values and religious beliefs.

Despite the efforts of the missionaries, the Kwakiutls continued to engage in traditional rituals. Potlatch ceremonies became even more important to the Kwakiutls. At the beginning of the 1800s, the potlatch was a small ceremony. Those attending a potlatch exchanged only a few dozen blankets. By the end of the century, the potlatch became a spectacular event during which chiefs displayed their wealth. Often, thousands of dollars' worth of goods were given away, and hundreds of people from different tribes would attend. The potlatch became the ceremonial focus of Kwakiutl society. ▲

CHAPTER **5**

The Potlatch Era

The word *potlatch* comes from the Nootka word *patshatl* (gift). Potlatch ceremonies were filled with feasting, speechmaking, and dancing, and they lasted for days. Among the Northwest Coast Indians, the Kwakiutls held the most lavish potlatches. They considered it a great honor to be generous to their guests.

Kwakiutl society was made up of groups of relatives who believed that they were descended from the same ancestor, often a spirit or a person once helped by a spirit. These extended families owned rights to specific hunting and fishing spots, the large house they shared, and the totem poles bearing their family crest symbols. Each group had its own sacred names, dances, and dramas that related its origins and history.

Within each group, there were many ranked positions. The holder of each position had special privileges, such as the right to hunt in a certain place or to wear a particular mask. These positions were passed on from one generation to the next, just as in European royal families. A Kwakiutl would assume several titles in his lifetime and inherit many new names. Names could be passed down from parents, along with all the honors earned by those who had held the name before.

One requirement of rank was to hold potlatches. Most of the Kwakiutls' wealth and labor went into potlatches, which were the main way to gain status. A host tried to give his guests more food and gifts than he had received at other potlatches. Because almost every Kwakiutl took part in potlatches, the celebrations created ties among all the Kwakiutl groups.

Charles Nowell, a Kwakiutl chief, wrote in his 1941 autobiography *Smoke from Their Fires* that his father told him,

In giving potlatches is the only good name you'll have when you grow up, but if you are careless and spend your money foolishly, then you'll . . . be one of the common people without any rank.

Potlatches were held to announce important events in a person's life. A single potlatch could go on for days and commemorate many different events. These events included birth, marriage, the assumption of a new rank, and death. Potlatches were also held when a family finished building a large house or raised a new totem pole. A new house had to be built and new totem poles carved every time one chief died and a new chief took his place. At a potlatch, the family crests and honors were officially transferred to the new house and chief.

At a large potlatch, people from neighboring villages would be invited. The hosts stood on the beach in their finest robes and headdresses, singing and dancing to greet the visitors as they approached by canoe. Sometimes large wooden figures were also set up to welcome them.

When guests arrived at a potlatch, they were announced and seated by rank. While they ate the huge feast that the host provided, a speaker explained the ancestral names of the food dishes and their history. The host then gave a grand speech in honor of the event. Masked dancers and singers acted out stories about the history of the host's family. Finally, the host distributed many valuable gifts to his guests. These gifts were considered payment for witnessing the speeches and family songs and accepting the claims made in them.

The potlatch had a strong religious meaning to the Kwakiutls. They believed that people could be wealthy only if they maintained good relations with the spirit world. Through potlatch rituals, the Kwakiutls showed respect to the spirits. The spirits were kind as long as people respected them.

To the Kwakiutls, spirits were not just figures to be honored on special occasions. They were deeply involved in everyday life. Every animal and plant had a spirit. The Kwakiutls believed that hunters could catch animals only because they wanted to be caught. The animal spirits did not mind if their bodies were eaten; they simply went home to the spirit world and put on a new body. These bodies were just the clothes the Animal People wore in the human world.

Hunters went to great lengths to please the animal spirits, especially the Salmon People. When the Kwakiutls caught salmon, they always thanked them and returned their bones to the water. They believed that the bones floated back to the Salmon People's house in the spirit world. If any were missing, the fish would be deformed when they returned or would be too angry to come back at all.

Even berries were believed to have spirits. The anthropologist Franz Boas wrote down the words of one berry picker:

> I have come, Supernatural-Ones, Long-Life-Makers, that I may take you, for that is the reason you have come. . . . Look! I come now dressed in my large basket and my small basket that you may go into it.

An untamed Cannibal Dancer at a Winter Ceremonial in Fort Rupert.

The main way spirits were honored, however, was through the *Winter Ceremonials*.
The Kwakiutls believed that winter was the
time of year when the spirits visited human
beings. They devoted months to elaborate
performances such as the ones they showed
Franz Boas. In 1895, Boas counted 53 different characters with roles in the Winter
Ceremonies. These ceremonies focused on
the initiation of young people into secret
dancing societies.

All Kwakiutls of high rank belonged to
dancing societies, each linked to a particular
spirit. These societies put on exciting shows
about the powers of their particular spirit
before the entire village. The right to join was
inherited. In the Cannibal Society, a senior
member had to retire before a relative could
begin the 12-year initiation process.

Many of the performances in the Winter
Ceremonies featured tricks and special effects. For instance, the masks the dancers
wore often had moving parts. The beak on a
Raven mask would open and close, and
other masks would slowly open to reveal a
different mask inside. Sometimes, people
dressed as spirits would fly down from the
roof on ropes. Other illusions included walking on water and using special gloves and

shoes to walk on fire or hold a flame in one's hands.

One performance that took a great deal of planning was the Ghost Dance. Secret tunnels were dug inside a house, and tubes made of seaweed were hidden beneath the floor. During the performance, a dancer pretended to visit the underworld, where the ghosts lived. Slowly, using the secret tunnels, he sank into the earth. Ghostly voices then rose out of the floor. These were actually men speaking into the hidden tubes from outside the house.

Kwakiutl society changed rapidly after the whites arrived. Trading with the newcomers increased the amount of wealth that could be given away at potlatches. Potlatches grew bigger and bigger. At the same time, the Kwakiutl population dropped dramatically due to disease. Between 1881 and 1921 the number of Kwakiutls fell from about 2,300 to about 1,100. Many chiefs and their relatives died in the epidemics. Often, there were no family members to inherit their positions.

People who once had no chance to claim a high rank now could. Those with enough money competed for the open positions by holding potlatches. Because of the growing competition and the increasing amounts of wealth involved, the years between 1881 and 1921 became known as the potlatch era.

Many potlatches continued to be small affairs. But a large potlatch may have cost the host's family as much as $40,000. Family members sometimes worked hard year-round at several jobs to pay for these extravagant displays. They would pool their earnings for years or even decades in order to hold a major potlatch.

Potlatch hosts gave away food, blankets, fur robes, cedar-bark mats, canoes, and other items. Modern goods obtained through trade, such as sewing machines, outboard motors, pool tables, furniture, cooking sets, and musical instruments, were also popular. To show how rich they were, some hosts began burning their property. Giant heaps of valuable goods were set on fire. The next family that held a potlatch would burn even more things to prove that they were richer than the first family.

Canadian authorities thought potlatches were wasteful and foolish. As the potlatches grew bigger, the authorities vowed to end potlatches as part of an official program "for the improvement and control of the Indians." Although all Northwest Coast Indian groups

continued on page 65

MAGICAL OBJECTS

The Kwakiutls believed that spirits with special powers visited them during the winter. In a series of rituals called the Winter Ceremonials, these spirits passed on their powers to members of secret societies.

Performances at the Winter Ceremonials were filled with magic tricks and theatrical effects. Statues seemed to speak and move, and objects appeared to fly through the air. Some participants seemed to walk on water or hold fire in their hands. Sometimes, people would appear to be killed, only to come back to life.

The photographs on the following pages show objects that were actually used in the Kwakiutls' Winter Ceremonials. Many represent spirits and have moving parts, such as mouths that open and close. One mask opens to reveal another mask inside.

All of these objects were collected between 1897 and 1904 by George Hunt, who was part Tlingit Indian. The collection is now owned by the American Museum of Natural History in New York City.

A ceremonial bowl in the shape of a spoon, the handle of which represents Dzonokwa. A giant female monster, Dzonokwa was said to wander through the woods, where she kidnapped and ate children. She also had the power to bestow great wealth on people.

The mask of a fool dancer, one of the performers who kept order during the Cannibal dance. The long nose is an allusion to the A'lasiamk, supernaturals with huge noses who were thought to grant the fool dancers their power.

58

People imbued with the power of the Cannibal-at-the-North-End-of-the-World exhibited wild behavior that, through the Winter Ceremonials, members of the Cannibal Society sought to tame. Rattles in the shape of human skulls such as these were shaken by the assistants of Cannibal Society initiates to calm them.

A mask representing the assistants of the Cannibal-at-the-North-End-of-the-World, Ho'xuhok (a cranelike being), and two ravens. The beaks of the three avian creatures could be moved to clack in rhythm as the wearer danced.

The simple, subtly hued raven mask
(above) dramatically opens to reveal another being, the brilliantly colored Raven
of the Sea (right). Initiates into the Cannibal Society would often become uncontrol-
lable at the sight of raven masks because
of the raven's close association with the
Cannibal-at-the-North-End-of-the-World.

A mask representing Sisiutl, an assistant of a female warrior named Tooquid. A snakelike creature, Sisiutl is shown to have a serpent's head at both of its ends and a human face at its center. The creature was thought to have the power to turn enemies to stone with its gaze.

A feast bowl in the shape of a two-headed wolf. Each wolf head holds in its teeth a Copper, an important Kwakiutl ceremonial object.

A mask composed of two octopus heads, one on top of the other. By manipulating the strings, which were probably invisible in the dark, the wearer could move the tentacles and open and shut the smaller head's mouth.

63

Wooden puppets depicting a ghost dancer and its two children.
These beings, who could bring the dead to life, were associates of
Tooquid. The puppets were manipulated during her dance to signify
her otherworldly powers.

Continued from page 56

were affected, the Kwakiutls became the government's main target.

Despite occasional arrests, the Kwakiutls continued to conduct both potlatches and the Winter Ceremonials in secret for years. In 1921, a huge potlatch was held near Alert Bay. More than 300 guests from almost every Kwakiutl village attended it. This turned out to be the last grand potlatch.

Afterward, 80 highly ranked Indians from all the tribes of the Kwakiutl Nation were arrested. Thirty were sentenced to jail for periods ranging from two months to a year. The other 50 defendants were released. But they had to give the authorities their ceremonial items—including masks and costumes—and promise never to hold potlatches again.

These events nearly killed the potlatching system among the Kwakiutls. A few still practiced the ritual, but they were very careful. They moved to more isolated areas to conduct the ceremonies. Or they held potlatches at the same time as Christmas and other Christian holidays to avoid detection. Other Kwakiutls abandoned the potlatch entirely.

Many people, such as missionaries, actually thought they were helping the Indians by

*Gifts at a women's
potlatch in 1898.*

forcing them to give up their old culture and adopt a new one. They considered this progress. But as one Kwakiutl chief told Franz Boas:

> Do we ask the white man, "Do as the Indian does?" No, we do not. Why then do you ask us, "Do as the white man does?" It is a strict law that bids us dance. It is a strict law that bids us distribute our property among our friends and neighbors. It is a good law. Let the white man observe his law. We shall observe ours. ▲

Nella Nelson, a Kwakiutl woman who teaches native studies in Victoria.

CHAPTER **6**

The Kwakiutls Today

Despite the Canadian government's battle against the potlatch, the Kwakiutls led relatively comfortable lives in the early 1900s. Many Kwakiutls made money by selling the fish that they caught. Others found work in canneries, on logging crews, and on farms.

In the 1920s, however, life became much harder for the Kwakiutls. Pollution and over-fishing caused a quick drop in the salmon population. Many Kwakiutls lost their jobs in the canneries. At the same time, non-Indians using large, expensive motorboats caught most of the remaining fish. Few Kwakiutls could afford to buy these boats.

The Kwakiutls could no longer make their living by fishing, as they had for hundreds of years. The depression that wrecked the world economy during the 1930s made things even worse. Without potlatches, it was harder for families to share what they had with one another. Kwakiutl villages suffered through years of poverty and despair.

Government agencies created to hear Indians' complaints instead allowed whites to continue stealing their land. The Indians formed new associations to fight for their legal rights. In response, the Canadian government made it a crime for these groups to raise or spend money on legal claims against the government. Political activists were not allowed to leave the reserves.

Groups such as the Allied Tribes of British Columbia and the Pacific Coast Native Fishermen's Association did have some victories. They persuaded the government to provide more money and services to needy Indians. They also won some hunting and fishing rights. But the government still rejected the Indians' claims to ownership of their ancestral lands.

The Canadian government eventually decided to reform its Indian policy. The Indian Act of 1951 granted Indians the right to vote, but only if they moved off the reserve and removed their names from the official list of Kwakiutl Indians. The new law also finally made it legal for the Kwakiutls to give potlatches again. By the early 1960s, the Kwakiutl population had grown to about 2,500 from its all-time low of 1,100 in the early 1920s. Many young Kwakiutls chose to move away from the smaller, more remote communities. Most settled in one of four large Kwakiutl villages: Alert Bay, Fort Rupert, Cape Mudge, and Kingcome Inlet. These villages offered the Indians schools, better health care, and more job opportunities.

Those who remained in smaller villages suffered from many problems, including poverty, malnutrition, and alcohol abuse. In the large villages, the Kwakiutls had to cope with crime, racism, and unemployment. The Canadian government finally had to face these problems when, in 1958, a white scholar named Harry Hawthorn wrote a report strongly criticizing the unfair treatment of the Indians.

Charges that the Indians had made for years could no longer be ignored. The government soon provided better medical care, education, and unemployment insurance. Many Kwakiutls who worked off the reserve could now afford to return home and make their living from fishing. New government

programs supported the Indians' efforts to improve their own lives and govern themselves.

The Kwakiutls are now organized into 14 bands, which are independent and self-governing. Their councils provide electricity, housing, fire prevention, and road maintenance. Some offer education and job training, and many have even started businesses such as restaurants, hotels, and laundromats.

Linguist Peter Wilson teaches his class how to pronounce the Kwakiutls' native language, Kwakwala.

Because many Kwakiutls feel that non-Indian schools serve their children poorly, several bands have started their own school programs. In addition to the usual subjects, these schools offer training in fishing, forestry, and carpentry. These courses provide the Kwakiutls with job skills that they can use in their communities.

Kwakiutl children are also learning the traditional religious ceremonies from their elders. Today, potlatches and other rituals celebrate the building of houses and community centers, the raising of totem poles, and the opening of the fishing season. These rituals, along with secret society initiations, have once again become central to Kwakiutl life.

Kwakiutl artists are thriving as well. Many wonderful examples of Kwakiutl art, old and new, can be found in museums around the world. Modern Kwakiutl art is highly desired by non-Indian art collectors. As a result, artists can earn as much in a few months of carving as they could in a year of fishing.

Many of the art masterpieces that were taken after the 1921 potlatch arrests were recently returned to the Kwakiutls. Two museums were opened to house these items. These museums, located in Alert Bay and Cape Mudge, also serve as social and educational centers. They provide art, language, and ceremonial programs. Since most Kwakiutls speak English now, these classes are needed to keep their language, Kwakwala, from becoming extinct.

During the 1980s, the Kwakiutls joined with other tribes of coastal British Columbia to continue fighting for their legal rights. Because much of their land was take from them

Agnes Alfred carries on the Kwakiutl tradition of basket weaving.

illegally, they believe it still belongs to them. They want to be paid for logging, fishing, and mineral rights. Their claims are attracting worldwide attention and sympathy.

Although they do business with the outside world, many Kwakiutls want to remain as independent as possible. The Kwakiutls are proud that they have preserved some of their traditional ways. But they also seek respect and equality in the non-Indian world.

Over a hundred years ago, Franz Boas wrote: "I often ask myself what advantages our 'good society' has over that of the 'savages' and find, the more I see of their customs, that we have no right to look down upon them." In the past, the Kwakiutls were studied only by anthropologists. Today, more and more people are learning to respect and admire the unique society created by the Indians of the Northwest Coast. ◭

CHRONOLOGY

1778 English captain James Cook trades with Indians in Nootka Sound

1792 English explorer George Vancouver arrives at Cape Mudge, becoming the first European known to visit a Kwakiutl village

1849 Hudson's Bay Company builds a trading post in Kwakiutl territory at Fort Rupert, which quickly becomes the center of Kwakiutl trade

1850s Gold is discovered in the Pacific Northwest, and thousands of non-Indians arrive on Vancouver Island

1865 British gunboats shell Kwakiutl village at Fort Rupert

1876 The Canadian government passes the Indian Act, which outlaws most of the Kwakiutls' social and religious practices, including the potlatch

1886 Anthropologist Franz Boas pays his first visit to the Kwakiutls at the village of Newhitty

1921 The Canadian government arrests 80 high-ranking Kwakiutls for participating in a potlatch near the village of Alert Bay

1936 The Kwakiutls create the Pacific Coast Native Fishermen's Association

1951 A revision of the Indian Act lifts the ban on potlatches

1979–80 Kwakiutl museums open at Cape Mudge and Alert Bay

GLOSSARY

allotment a policy of the Canadian government in the 1880s aimed at breaking up Indian land into small, privately owned plots; also, one of these plots

anthropologist a scientist who studies human beings and the different ways in which they live

breechcloth an article of clothing made of cloth or leather and worn around the waist

copper a ceremonial copper shield of great value to the Kwakiutls. A typical shield might be worth 500 blankets.

crest symbol an image of a spirit to whom one's ancestors are spiritually connected

epidemic an outbreak of disease that spreads through a region, affecting large numbers of people

missionary a follower of a particular religion who attempts to convert others to his or her faith

potlatch a ceremony of feasting, speechmaking, and dancing, during which the host gives away possessions to show his rank and wealth

reserve an area of land set aside for use by Indians

totem pole a post carved with a series of figures and symbols that tell important stories in a family's history

Winter Ceremonial a complex series of rituals held by the Kwakiutls in the winter; the Ceremonials used dancing, stagecraft, and magic tricks to show the powers of spirits

INDEX

INDEX

ABOUT THE AUTHOR

G. S. PRENTZAS is an editor and writer who lives in New York City.

PICTURE CREDITS